SWEET
HERBS
AND
SUNDRY
FLOWERS

SWEET HERBS AND SUNDRY FLOWERS

Medieval
Gardens and
the Gardens of
The Cloisters

by
Tania Bayard

The Metropolitan Museum of Art
New York
David R. Godine, Publisher
Boston

Initial funding for this book was generously provided by the
Garden Committee of The Cloisters.

Published by The Metropolitan Museum of Art, New York,
in association with David R. Godine, Publisher, Inc.,
306 Dartmouth Street, Boston, Massachusetts 02116

Produced by the Department of Special Publications,
The Metropolitan Museum of Art
Typeset by U.S. Lithograph Inc., New York
Printed and bound by Kingsport Press, Kingsport, Tennessee
Designed by Linda Florio
First edition

Library of Congress Cataloging in Publication Data
Bayard, Tania.
    Sweet herbs and sundry flowers.
    Bibliography: p.
    1. Cloisters Gardens (New York, N.Y.) 2. Gardens,
Medieval — New York (N.Y.) 3. Herb gardens — New York
(N.Y.) 4. Gardening — Europe — History. 5. Herbs.
I. Title.
SB466.U7C563   1985   712'.7   85-7133
ISBN 0-87099-422-0
ISBN 0-87923-593-4 (Godine)

The cover shows a detail of "The Unicorn in Captivity," one of a
series of seven tapestries entitled *The Hunt of the Unicorn*; silk,
wool, and metal thread; French or Flemish, ca. 1500. Gift of John
D. Rockefeller, Jr., 1937   37.80.6

Ful gay was al the ground, and queint,
And powdred, as men had it peint,
With many a fressh and sondry flowr,
That casten up ful good savour.

From *The Romance of the Rose*,
translated by Geoffrey Chaucer

FOREWORD

If you have walked through a wood of wild ginger,
forget-me-nots, and unfurling ferns, or wandered in a
meadow of strawberries, yarrow, and oxeye daisies, you
have had the opportunity to admire medieval plants.
Sweet Herbs and Sundry Flowers is an introduction to
medieval plants and gardening practices by way of the
gardens of The Cloisters. In her work as assistant
horticulturist at The Cloisters, Tania Bayard has become aware of the many questions visitors ask about
medieval gardening. Tania addresses those questions
here, providing a list of the plants in The Cloisters'
gardens. Her book has long been needed, and I am
pleased that Tania, who left a career in art history to
become a horticulturist, shares her knowledge and
experience with us.

Gardening is an art shaped by the gardener, using a
palette of light, water, soil, special living matter, and
time. For modern medieval gardeners historical time is
also a factor. Plant lists from medieval sources must be
consulted and plant names checked against those found
in taxonomic encyclopedias and guides to European
flora. At The Cloisters, seeds for medieval annuals,
biennials, and perennials are ordered from North
American seed companies and through seed catalogues
from European botanic gardens. We are not always
easily able to find what we need. Some seeds are hard to
locate and are therefore in our "rare" category; other
medieval species of seeds are not commonly grown and
are unavailable from regular commercial companies;
still other plants may have no long-term ornamental

value in a display garden, may be of a sprawling rampant nature unbecoming in a small garden, or may have special requirements that make them difficult to grow.

Seed orders are completed during the months of December and January. The seeds are sown in flats in a greenhouse, and after the last spring frost the young seedlings are planted in the cloistered gardens. Once the plants come into bloom their flowers, leaves, and fruits are gathered for comparison with medieval plant descriptions. Frequently a fake — a plant assumed, until it flowers, to be a medieval species — is found. Several years ago we planted seeds for the clove-pink carnation (*Dianthus caryophyllus*), which has a lovely clove-scented flower that is depicted in the Unicorn Tapestries. When the plants came into bloom their flowers were deep pink with dark burgundy centers. Clearly here was a different species. Our search for the true seed had to begin again.

Many people want to grow medieval plants in their own gardens, where they can enjoy the smells, textures, and colors throughout the growing season. Whether your "garden" is a shady plot of sweet woodruff and primroses, a sunny backyard of Madonna lilies, cabbage roses, and lavender, or only a pot of parsley, you can easily grow and enjoy medieval plants. Take note of the Latin and common names of plants that attract you; a catalogue of old varieties of seeds and a gardening book will guide you the rest of the way.

The delight in reading *Sweet Herbs and Sundry Flowers* is the realization that the modern gardener's experience is not unlike that of gardeners one thousand years ago. Then, as now, garden plots were selected for adequate light and water drainage, the soil was prepared in the spring, noxious weeds and stones were removed, the ground was tilled and raked, and cow manure was added for fertilizer. Seeds and young plants were lovingly tended. When the plants were mature, roots, stems, leaves, flowers, and fruits were harvested for food, medicines, and various household uses. Following the fall harvest, the ground was readied for winter, and thoughts of spring were always present. How wonderful it is that we share with the medieval gardener the same labors and joys, getting our hands dirty with soil as did the ninth-century monk, Walahfrid Strabo.

Susan Taylor Leach
Horticulturist, The Cloisters

ACKNOWLEDGMENTS

I should like to thank the many people who helped in the preparation of this book. Above all, I owe a debt of gratitude to Charles D. Webster and the other members of the Garden Committee of The Cloisters, without whose enthusiastic support *Sweet Herbs and Sundry Flowers* would never have come to be. I am also deeply indebted to my good friend Susan Leach, Cloisters Horticulturist, who labored with me for many hours over the plant list, read the manuscript several times, and offered constant reassurance, always with a sense of humor. Other members of The Cloisters staff — William Wixom, Jane Hayward, Timothy Husband, Nancy Kueffner, Carl Koivuniemi, and Robert Goldsmith — read the manuscript and made helpful suggestions. David Kiehl of the Department of Prints and Photographs at The Metropolitan Museum of Art made several excellent recommendations concerning the illustrations. Frank Anderson, honorary curator of Rare Books and Manuscripts at the New York Botanical Garden, and John Harvey, president of the Garden History Society, read the manuscript with great care and advised me on a number of points. Steven K-M. Tim, director of Scientific Affairs at the Brooklyn Botanic Garden, and Holly Shimizu, curator of The National Herb Garden, checked the plant list and made recommendations concerning the taxonomy. I am extremely grateful for the help all these people have given me.

I consider myself fortunate to have worked with two very special people in the preparation of this book. Linda Florio, the designer, has been delightfully inventive with the illustrations, and Barbara Anderman, my editor, has guided me through the publication process with rare intelligence and patience.

Special thanks are due to my husband, Robert Cammarota, who carefully read and reread the manuscript. His good judgment and meticulous attention to detail have been invaluable, as have his understanding and good humor. I dedicate this book to him.

CONTENTS

And all thy cloisters smell of apple
    orchards,
And there are lilies white and small
    red roses,
And every bird sings in the early
    morning. . . .

             Lament for Alcuin,
                ninth century[1]

INTRODUCTION

The gardens of The Cloisters bloom in a unique museum, a division of The Metropolitan Museum of Art, designed to suggest the layout of a medieval European monastery. Planted in reconstructed Romanesque and Gothic cloisters, the gardens resemble those that provided bodily sustenance and spiritual refreshment for monks of centuries ago.

The gardens help to set the tone of the Museum. The Cuxa Cloister garden, a haven of sunlight, brightly colored flowers, bird song, and splashing water, is the focal point of the main-floor galleries. The Trie Cloister contains a garden of plants depicted in the Unicorn Tapestries that hang in the Museum; here small birds come to drink from a fountain just as they do in the late-Gothic hangings after which the garden was designed. The Bonnefont Cloister garden is fragrant with the household herbs grown in the gardens of the Middle Ages. The views over the walls that border the Bonnefont garden on two sides are spectacular, revealing the Museum's dramatic situation on ledges high above Fort Tryon Park and the Hudson River. The Cloisters, like its medieval predecessors, is walled and self-contained. Within the monastic enclosure, gardens were essential for survival.

The gardens enhance the setting in which The Cloisters' collection of medieval art is displayed and broaden the visitor's understanding of life in the Middle Ages. James J. Rorimer, curator of the Department of Medieval Art at the time The Cloisters was planned and built, took an active interest in the gardens and supervised their design and the choice of plants. He was aided by Margaret B. Freeman, who did extensive research on the history and symbolism of the plants of the Middle Ages. When the Museum opened in 1938, with Mr. Rorimer in charge, the gardens were one of its major attractions, and they continue to be so today.

With the exception of some of the flowers in the Cuxa Cloister, where modern varieties have been included to ensure continuous bloom throughout the summer, all the species of plants in the gardens were known in the Middle Ages — a time period extending roughly from the fourth century to the early fifteenth century in Italy and to the early sixteenth century in northern Europe.

The gardens are maintained by a horticultural staff engaged in research as well as gardening. As new information on gardening practices and plants of the Middle Ages becomes available, the gardens are further developed. Containing over two hundred and fifty species of herbs, flowers, and trees, the gardens of The Cloisters comprise one of the most important specialized plant collections in the world.

GARDENING IN THE MIDDLE AGES

If you do not let laziness clog
Your labor, if you do not insult with
  misguided efforts
The gardener's multifarious wealth,
  and if you do not
Refuse to harden or dirty your
  hands in the open air
Or to spread whole baskets of dung
  on the sun-parched soil —
Then, you may rest assured, your
  soil will not fail you.

Walahfrid Strabo,
ninth century[2]

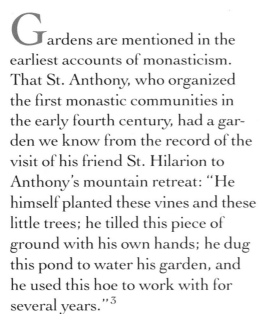

Gardens are mentioned in the earliest accounts of monasticism. That St. Anthony, who organized the first monastic communities in the early fourth century, had a garden we know from the record of the visit of his friend St. Hilarion to Anthony's mountain retreat: "He himself planted these vines and these little trees; he tilled this piece of ground with his own hands; he dug this pond to water his garden, and he used this hoe to work with for several years."[3]

Two centuries later, when St. Benedict, founder of the monastic order that bears his name, codified the rules under which communities of monks lived, he made special mention of gardens. St. Benedict's Rule, which governed monastic life throughout the Middle Ages, speci-

fied that "If it can be done, the monastery should be so established that all the necessary things, such as water, mill, garden and various workshops, may be within the enclosure, so that there is no necessity for the monks to go about outside of it, since that is not at all profitable for their souls."[4]

Our knowledge of monastic as well as secular gardens is nevertheless meager until the ninth century, when suddenly, with three remarkable documents, the picture of gardens and gardeners of the Middle Ages comes into focus.

The first of these documents is a decree, issued for Charlemagne before the year 812, that includes a list of eighty-nine species of plants he wanted grown in the imperial gardens throughout his empire.[5] The modern gardener is familiar with many of them — radishes, carrots, lettuce, and cucumbers, for example — but others, such as orach, madder, costmary, and lovage sound delightfully medieval.

The second document includes the earliest-known garden ground plans. These are part of the oldest surviving plan of a monastery (c. 816–20), an idealized scheme designed as a model for builders of Benedictine abbeys. On this plan, which is preserved today at the Abbey of St. Gall in Switzerland, the monastery is conceived as a large group of buildings with the church at the center, flanked by a cloister on its south side. Around this cloister are the monks' dormitory, refectory (dining hall), and cellar. Many other buildings, including the

abbot's house, infirmary, kitchens, guesthouses, school, barns, and workshops, surround this core.

The St. Gall plan includes several gardens, all essential to the daily life of the monastery. The cloister garth, centrally located, was a place for the monks to enjoy the fresh air. The kitchen garden supplied vegetables and herbs for the monks' table. The infirmary garden provided the herbs used in medicines prepared by the monks' physician. The cemetery was a garden of sorts, too, for fruit and nut trees were planted there. Fields of cereal and root crops, as well as vineyards and orchards, which need-ed larger growing spaces, would have been cultivated on farm lands outside the walls of the monastery; these are not shown on the plan.

The gardens on the St. Gall plan are similar to those represented in art and literature throughout the Middle Ages. Enclosed on four sides by arcades or walls, they appear tidy and symmetrical. The cloister

lawn is divided into quadrants by crossed paths, while in the kitchen and infirmary gardens crops are grown in evenly spaced rows of rectangular beds. On the St. Gall plan these beds are labeled with the names of some of the plants com-monly grown in medieval gardens: celery, coriander, dill, lettuce, and garlic are among those in the kitchen garden; sage, rue, fennel, mint, roses, and lilies are included in the infirmary garden.

The third source from the ninth century is a firsthand account of the horticultural efforts of a medieval monk. Around the year 840, Walahfrid Strabo, abbot of Reichenau (on Lake Constance), wrote a long poem dedicated to his garden. Walahfrid "the squint-eyed" was an important and original scholar, humanist, and poet, but it is for the *Hortulus*, or "Little Garden," that he is best known today. Walahfrid loved watering, weeding, and getting his hands dirty in the soil, and in his poem he described the pleasures and hard work of gardening. To our delight we learn that his experiences were the same as ours. He spread manure, tore up weeds, routed moles, and encouraged worms. He had a true gardener's enthusiasm for his work and a poet's sensitivity to the beauty of his plants. He wrote that his garden was one of the greatest joys of his cloistered life. Eleven hundred years later, we know exactly what he meant.

Walahfrid's was a typical medieval garden, probably very much like the kitchen and infirmary gardens on the St. Gall plan, surrounded by a wall and compartmentalized into rectangular beds that were raised from the ground and faced with planks. Gardens like this were often represented in medieval manuscript paintings. The types of enclosures varied — walls, fences, trellises, or hedges were used — and gardens were often embellished with turf benches, arbors, trained trees, and

other refinements. In general, however, medieval gardens were enclosed and subdivided into geometric units. The plants were contained in even rows of rectangular beds, the paths were straight and at right angles to each other, and there was usually a fountain or other water source at the center. Although they lacked the informality we are accustomed to in modern gardens, medieval gardens were places of delight, often beautifully described by poets and writers, such as, for instance, Boccaccio, in his mid-fourteenth-century book of tales, the *Decameron*.

> After this they went into a walled garden beside the mansion, which at first glance seemed to them so beautiful that they began to examine it more carefully in detail. On its outer edges and through the centre ran wide walks as straight as arrows, covered with pergolas of vines which gave every sign of bearing plenty of grapes that year. . . . The sides of these walks were almost closed in with jasmin and red and white roses, so that it was possible to walk in the garden in a perfumed and delicious shade, un-

touched by the sun, not only in the early morning, but when the sun was high in the sky. . . . In the midst of this garden was something which they praised even more than all the rest; this was a lawn of very fine grass, so green that it seemed nearly black, coloured with perhaps a thousand kinds of flowers. This lawn was shut in with very green citron and orange trees bearing at the same time both ripe fruit and young fruit and flowers, so that they pleased the sense of smell as well as charmed the eyes with shade. And in the midst of this lawn was a fountain of very white marble most marvellously carved.[6]

The making of such an elegant garden would have required horticultural expertise of a high order. In fact, by the thirteenth century, the practice of ornamental gardening was very advanced. Around 1260 Albertus Magnus, the great Dominican theologian and scientist, wrote a treatise, *On Vegetables and Plants*, in which he gave instructions on the setting out of a pleasure garden. The first requirement was a lawn, "for the sight is in no way so pleasantly refreshed as by fine and close grass kept short." He gives elaborate instructions for preparing the soil and planting a lawn where the grass will eventually "cover the surface like a green cloth." Around this lawn are to be planted "every sweet-smelling herb such as rue, and sage and basil, and likewise all sorts of flowers, as the violet, columbine, lily, rose, iris and the like." There should be a bench of flowering turf, a fountain, and "sweet trees, with perfumed flowers and agreeable shade, like grapevines, pears, apples, pomegranates, sweet bay trees, cypresses and such like."[7]

Medieval gardening techniques were surprisingly sophisticated. Young plants were grown in nurseries, the art of grafting was highly refined, rare and unusual plants were cultivated, and gardeners exchanged plants, seeds, and cuttings. Gardeners used implements very similar to our own, with the exception of power tools. They also had instruction books. One of the most popular of these was written

around 1300 in Italy by a retired Bolognese lawyer, Petrus de Crescentiis. His treatise, *Opus ruralium commodorum* (The Advantages of Country Living), was a working manual on botany, animal husbandry, beekeeping, and many other aspects of farming and gardening. A compilation of much existing knowledge on agriculture, the book was immensely successful. It went into numerous editions and was translated into several languages (although, unfortunately, not into English), proving that medieval people were just as eager to improve their gardening skills as we are today.[8]

12

One of the most delightful medieval treatises on the art of gardening was written at the end of the fourteenth century. The author, the *Ménagier de Paris* (Householder, or Goodman, of Paris), was an elderly middle-class burgher who had taken a very young wife.[9] Because he felt that his inexperienced bride needed training in household management, he wrote a book of instruction to guide her in overseeing his servants,

marketing, cooking, cleaning, entertaining, and gardening. The book gives a fascinating picture of domestic arrangements in the Middle Ages. Since plants entered into many of the daily operations of this bourgeois household — from cooking to ridding the house of vermin — the Goodman of Paris devoted a chapter of his book to gardening. His knowledge of the subject was sound. He admonished his wife not to water in the heat of the sun; to water only the stems and the earth, not the leaves; to thin young lettuce plants; to throw sawdust on anthills to get rid of the ants; to place cinders underneath cabbages to kill caterpillars; and not to let greens go to seed. He knew that when plants have wintered over in the cellar they should not be brought too quickly into the dry summer air; that dead branches of sage should be cut off in winter; that marjoram should not be grown in the shade; and that plenty of earth should be

left around the roots of vegetables when they are transplanted.

Medieval gardeners were very much like gardeners of today. A late-fourteenth-century French conversation manual attributed the following statement to a gardener who was asked how much he had earned:

> I have grafted all the trees in my garden with the fairest grafts that I have seen for a long while, and they are beginning to put forth green; also I have dug another garden and I have very carefully planted cabbages, porray,° parsley and sage and other goodly herbs; and furthermore I have pulled up and cleared away from it all the nettles, brambles and wicked weeds, and I have sown it full well with many good seeds; and in it I have likewise many fair trees bearing divers fruits, such as apples, pears, plums, cherries and nuts, and everywhere have I very well looked after them, and yet all I have earned this week is 3d. and my expenses....[10]

°vegetables such as beets, spinach, leeks, peas

THE USES
OF HERBS
IN THE
MIDDLE AGES

For the sickly take this wort rosemary, pound it with oil, smear the
sickly one, wonderfully thou healest
him.

Saxon ms. herbal[11]

I have heard that if maids will take
wild Tansy and lay it to soake in
Buttermilk for the space of nine
days and wash their faces therewith,
it will make them look very faire.

Master Jherom Brunswyke,
The Virtuose Boke of Distyllacion,
1527[12]

Walahfrid Strabo, writing in the ninth century about the Madonna lilies and roses in his garden, stressed their medicinal uses and symbolism as well as their beauty and fragrance. In the twentieth century we may find this strange, for we have largely forgotten the symbolism of plants, and we are not often aware of their importance in our medicines. Most of us do not know, as medieval

people did, how to use plants for clothing, dyes, cosmetics, perfumes, and insecticides, even though many of the common names of plants — boneset, birthwort, feverfew, self-heal, wolfsbane, soapwort, chaste tree, and lady's bedstraw — are descriptive of what they were used for in the past. The Madonna lily in Walahfrid's garden was both a symbol of Christian chastity and a potent medicine, for its crushed leaves and roots were used to cure snake bites, bruises, and leprosy. Walahfrid's rose, symbol of the Virgin and of martyrs, yielded an oil that was used for a variety of ailments, including headaches, dysentery, and fevers.

Many of the healing properties medieval people attributed to herbs are surprising. For example, we do not usually think of fennel, mint, and sage as medicinal plants, yet

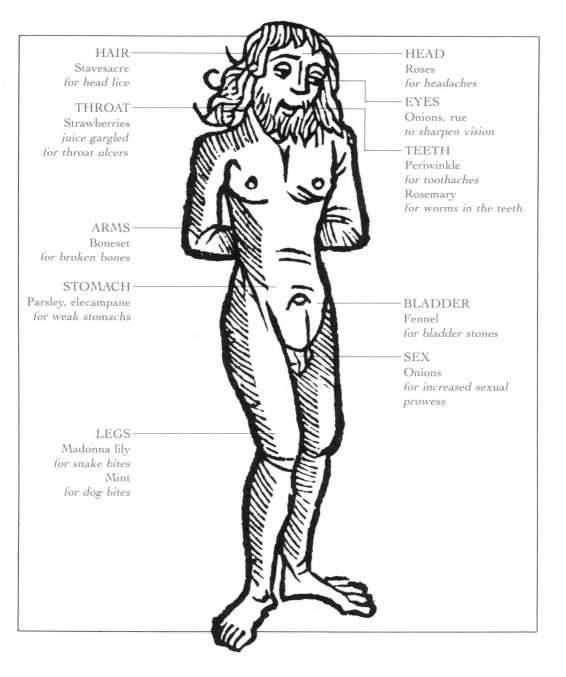

HAIR
Stavesacre
for head lice

THROAT
Strawberries
juice gargled
for throat ulcers

ARMS
Boneset
for broken bones

STOMACH
Parsley, elecampane
for weak stomachs

LEGS
Madonna lily
for snake bites
Mint
for dog bites

HEAD
Roses
for headaches

EYES
Onions, rue
to sharpen vision

TEETH
Periwinkle
for toothaches
Rosemary
for worms in the teeth

BLADDER
Fennel
for bladder stones

SEX
Onions
for increased sexual
prowess

during the Middle Ages these were all held to have wonderful curative powers. The *Tacuinum sanitatis*, an eleventh-century health handbook, tells us that fennel is good for the eyes, for fever, snake bites, and bladder stones; that mint cures abscesses, dog bites, and hiccups; and that sage is beneficial for nerves and paralysis. Sage, the author warns, also makes the hair fall out, but this can be remedied by washing the head with solutions containing two other familiar herbs, myrtle and saffron.[13]

Just about every herb known in the Middle Ages, whether cultivated in a garden or gathered from the wild, had at least one, and usually several, medicinal uses. Betony, for instance, according to Walahfrid and the herbalists, was good for just about everything. Rosemary is listed in an herbal of 1525 as a cure for asthma, evil swellings, cankers, gout, coughs, poisoning, worms in the teeth, and bad dreams.[14] Parsley was recommended for fever, heart pains, stitch, weak stomach, stones, and paralysis,[15] and onions were said to be good for the eyesight and for dog bites, skin discoloration, and baldness; they also cleared the head and increased sexual prowess.[16] The herbals tell us that periwinkle was supposed to cure toothaches and fevers and that concoctions containing strawberry juice could be gargled for throat ulcers. Some plants induced a general sense of well-being. Rue sharpened the vision, elecampane strengthened the stomach, dates made a sick person stronger, and quinces promoted

cheerfulness.[17] As for violets, one had only to smell them to feel better.

Herbs were very important in any medieval household. In an age of poor sanitation they were useful as disinfectants and insecticides. Rue, used since antiquity as a disin-fectant because of its strong, acrid smell, was strewn about to purify the air and to ward off disease. Albertus Magnus, the thirteenth-century theologian and scientist, also recommended planting rue among the other plants in a garden so that its powerful smell would discourage harmful vermin. Oint-ment made of the seeds of staves-acre (a relative of larkspur) was used to dispel head lice; wormwood and rosemary were laid away with clothes as moth repellents; penny-royal was scattered around homes to drive away fleas; and one book recommended the smoke of burning southernwood to drive snakes out of the house.[18] Pastes made of the powdered roots of aconite and hellebore, which contain deadly

poisons, were made into preparations to use against larger pests — rats, wolves, and foxes.[19] On occasion these poisons must have been used on people, too, for Walahfrid Strabo wrote that if a wicked stepmother poisoned your food with aconite, horehound would counteract it.

Flowers and sweet-smelling herbs had pleasanter uses. They were worn as garlands, they adorned altars and statues in churches, and they embellished private homes. Herbs freshened the air and gave their scents to perfumes, washing waters, and soaps. Aromatic plants such as fennel, rosemary, and sweet woodruff were strewn around homes and churches.[20] The petals of roses were placed in chests to make clothes fragrant, and Walahfrid noted that preparations of iris root stiffened linen and gave it a good scent as well. Many herbs were used cosmetically: rosemary boiled in white wine cleaned the face, crushed Madonna lily roots took away wrinkles and cured baldness, chamomile boiled with honey cleared the skin of blemishes, and the juice of catmint mixed with rose oil removed the scars left by wounds.

Herbs were employed in the making and dyeing of cloth. A well-known medieval image is that of the woman with a distaff, pulling strands of flax from a bundle of fibers to make linen. If the housewife worked with wool, she would use the dried seed heads of teasel, which are covered with hundreds of hooked spines,

to raise the nap, and other plants to dye it. One of the most widely used dyes was woad, the blue body-paint of the ancient people of Britain. This dye, extracted from the leaves of the woad plant, was used extensively in the manufacture of blue cloth. Weld, whose leaves, stems, and seeds yielded a bright yellow dye, and madder, from whose roots a red dye was obtained, were the other major dye plants. Combinations of dyes from woad, weld, and madder provided all the colors in the series of tapestries depicting the Hunt of the Unicorn, which hang in The Cloisters. Agrimony, lady's bedstraw, dyer's greenweed, and the tiny pollen-laden stigmas of the saffron crocus — more than four thousand to an ounce — were also sources of dyes in the Middle Ages.

Saffron provided artists with an imitation gold for their manuscript illuminations. The yellow juice of celandine combined with egg yolk and mercury produced another substitute for gold leaf. Artists obtained yellow from weld and green from the juices of iris flowers and honeysuckle berries. Woad was used for blue in manuscript and panel paintings. The seeds of flax supplied the linseed oil used as a medium in mixing paints and varnishes.[21]

Many herbs were, of course, used for food and seasoning. Some of the herbs grown for flavoring in medieval times are well known today — the Goodman of Paris had mint, sage, lavender, and marjoram, for example — but many other herbs that are little used now were common as seasonings in the Middle Ages. Hyssop added bitterness to omelettes, pickles, soups, and meat pies, while tansy, another bitter-tasting herb, was mixed with eggs

in tansy cakes and used in omelettes and salads. Dittany of Crete, a plant related to marjoram, was used for flavoring. People liked strong flavors; one fourteenth-century recipe for salad calls for a potent mixture of parsley, sage, garlic, onion, leek, borage, fennel, mint, cress, rue, rosemary, and purslane.[22]

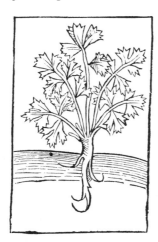

Mallow was considered a vegetable, the root of elecampane was made into a sweetmeat, and flowers were eaten as well. Marigolds, violets, primroses, and borage were added to salads and other dishes, and pinks gave the flavor of cloves to sauces, preserves, and drinks. Saffron, mint, sage, parsley, pot marigold, and other herbs were used as food dyes, for medieval people ate their meals vividly colored as well as highly seasoned.

Medieval gardens also included many vegetables that are staples in backyard gardens today — onions, leeks, radishes, parsley, lettuce, celery, parsnips, cucumbers, beans, peas, carrots, and melons. Other plants used as potherbs and in salads — dandelion and sorrel, for example — are not so commonly eaten today.

Fruit trees and vines, in addition to herbs, were essential to the medieval household. In monastic communities these were mostly planted in orchards and vineyards outside the monastery walls, but fruit trees were also sometimes grown in the cemeteries, within the confines of the monastery, and the monks could stroll in the shade of the branches. On the plan from St. Gall, apple, pear, and quince are among the fruit and nut trees found between the plots in the burial ground. Some kitchen gardens had a few fruit trees, whose crops were eaten fresh or used in cooking, as they are today. The quince was a popular fruit, used in sweet desserts and preserves. Apples and pears were eaten in a variety of ways and also made into cider or perry, a fermented drink.

Pears were good for weak stomachs, apples for overheated livers, and quinces for diarrhea, according to one author.[23] Hildegard of Bingen recommended the ashes of the grapevine soaked in wine for decaying gums and loose teeth.[24] Fruits, like all the other plants in the medieval garden, had many uses. But even though the gardens of the Middle Ages were basically utilitarian, the people who planted and cared for them were no less aware of the beauty of flowers and plants than we are today. The Goodman of Paris, who liked to see his young wife filling the house with herbs and branches, encouraged her to grow roses and violets and to weave garlands. Walahfrid Strabo, who composed the *Hortulus* to extol the practical virtues of his plants, also wrote poetically of golden melons ripening in the summer sun, snow-white lilies fragrant as incense, and poppy heads balanced on delicate stems. He dedicated the poem to his teacher, Grimald, abbot of St. Gall, whom he pictured sitting happily under the sun-dappled leaves of the fruit trees in his garden. This is an image we might well have of Walahfrid himself, and of all gardeners of the Middle Ages.

THE
GARDENS
OF THE
CLOISTERS

The lily is an herb with a white
flower. And though the leaves
of the flower be white yet within
shineth the likeness of gold.

Bartholomaeus Anglicus,
thirteenth century[25]

The Cloisters is built around architectural elements from the cloisters of several French monasteries. Within the Museum there are four cloisters, in part reconstructed, three of which contain outdoor gardens. Each of these gardens has a special character. In the Cuxa Cloister, on the main floor, there is a garth garden — an enclosed yard with trees, flowers, and grass. In a monastery this court, surrounded by covered walkways and open to the sky, would have been situated at the heart of the complex, a pleasant green space where the monks could stroll and meditate in the fresh air. The two gardens on the ground floor of the Museum are entirely different. The Bonnefont Cloister contains an herb garden that is representative of secular as well as monastic kitchen and infirmary gardens where vegetables, flowers, and plants used for seasonings, medicines, scents, and dyes

were grown. The garden in the Trie Cloister is pure fantasy. In it the plants and trees of the Unicorn Tapestries, exhibited in the Museum, are brought to life; all the plants were known in the Middle Ages, but no such garden ever existed. A fourth garden is a small indoor garden under the protective skylight of the Saint-Guilhem Cloister, on the main floor. This garden is planted only during the winter months, when the flowers of forced bulbs and other plants brighten the cloister with color and fragrance.

Many medieval sources were, and continue to be, consulted in the selection of plants for the gardens of The Cloisters. Among these are the *Hortulus* of Walahfrid Strabo, in which the monk lovingly described twenty-three plants he grew in his garden; Charlemagne's list of the plants he wanted grown in the imperial gardens; and the plan from

St. Gall, on which all thirty-four beds in the infirmary and vegetable gardens are labeled with the names of plants to be grown in each. The treatise on agriculture by Petrus de Crescentiis and the chapter on gardening in the book of domestic instruction by the Goodman of Paris also contain valuable information on the contents of medieval gardens.

Additional sources of information are medieval translations of *De materia medica* (The Materials of Medicine) by Dioscorides, a Greek work of the first century A.D. that was considered the definitive source of information on the medicinal uses of plants throughout the Middle Ages;[26] the *Physica* (Natural Science) of the twelfth-century abbess, Hildegard of Bingen; and many medieval herbals — books of plant lore and plant use going back to antiquity.

Plants and gardens are often depicted in medieval works of art. One well-known example is the Book of Hours painted for Anne of Brittany by Jean Bourdichon in the early sixteenth century, which has borders embellished with more than three hundred plants, all labeled and portrayed as realistically as if copied from nature. Within The Cloisters collection itself there are many representations of plants, from the patterns of ivy and bryony decorating Gothic lusterware dishes to

the flower-filled backgrounds of late Gothic tapestries. The tapestries depicting the Hunt of the Unicorn are especially rich in flora; over one hundred species of flowers, trees, and shrubs, most of them identifiable, crowd the seven scenes. Plants have symbolic as well as decorative significance in these and in many other works of art in the Museum. In the Annunciation panel of the fifteenth-century Mérode altarpiece by Robert Campin, a Madonna lily holds a key position because it symbolizes the purity of the Virgin. A rose bush growing in the donor's garden in another panel of the same altarpiece foreshadows the coming martyrdom of Christ, while grapevines on Eucharistic vessels in the Museum treasury suggest both the blood of the Savior and the wine. In a fifteenth-century stained glass window in the Boppard room, St. Dorothea holds a large basket of red roses. According to legend, this martyr was able, after her execution, to have roses miraculously brought by an angel to one of her persecutors.

Capitals and other architectural elements throughout the Museum abound in leaves, vines, and flowers. Medieval sculptors often depicted plants for the beauty of their forms alone, as seen in the leaves of acanthus, palm, and grape, some stylized, others naturalistic, on the capitals in the Saint-Guilhem and Cuxa cloisters. A Gothic capital exhibited in the passageway of the Cuxa Cloister, near the entrance to the Early Gothic Hall, is decorated with the buds and flowers of mallow, as keenly observed as though the sculptor had copied a living plant.

Most of the flora found in the art works in the Museum grow in the gardens of The Cloisters. Simpler and more delicate than the showy hybrids of today, these are old varieties, the same that inspired artists centuries ago. Medieval artists often copied plants from pattern books or manuscripts, but they probably also imitated nature. The French art historian, Emile Mâle, wrote a beautiful passage describing the medieval artist

> creating the magnificent flora that came to life under his hand. . . . On the first day of spring he goes into some forest of the Ile-de-France, where humble plants are beginning to push through the earth. The fern tightly rolled like a powerful spring still has its downy covering, but by the side of the streams the arum is almost ready to open. He gathers the buds and the opening leaves, and gazes at them with the tender and passionate interest felt by all men in early youth, and which is the artist's birthright through life. The vigorous lines of these young plants which stretch upwards and aspire to be, seem to him full of strength and grandeur by their suggestion of concentrated energy. With an opening bud he makes the ornament which terminates a pinnacle, and with shoots pushing through the earth he decorates the cushion of a capital.[27]

THE
CUXA CLOISTER
GARTH GARDEN

Before St. Mary's house on the far
side of the threshold is the garden,
well-nursed, well-watered, and
lovely. About it there are walls,
boughs swinging every way; it
glows under the light, like an earthly
Paradise.

Tenth-century description
of a garden at the
monastery at Reichenau[28]

The plan of a typical medieval monastery included a central cloister whose covered and arcaded passageways surrounded a garth, an enclosed courtyard, open to the sky. Situated at the center of the monastic complex, the cloister and its garth gave access to the buildings arranged around them — the church and the monks' living, sleeping, and dining quarters. Usually the garth was on the south side of the church where it would receive the full warmth of the sun. On the plan from St. Gall, the oldest surviving plan of a monastery, the cloister garth is bounded on the north by the church, on the south by the refectory, on the east by the dormitory, and on the west by storage buildings. At The Cloisters there is no church, but the Cuxa garth is centrally located, linking the main-floor galleries.

The architecture of the Cuxa Cloister is a reconstruction, about

one-quarter the original size, of the Romanesque cloister from the Benedictine monastery of Saint-Michel-de-Cuxa, in the northeastern Pyrenees. Its covered walkways and arcades with twelfth-century capitals surround a garden with crossed paths, a central fountain, lawns in the quadrants, and rich plantings of flowers and trees (see the diagram on page 43). It is not known what was planted in the medieval garth at Cuxa. In fact, historical evidence of flower gardens in medieval cloister garths is lacking.[29] Flowers were grown in other types of monastic gardens, however — Walahfrid's lilies and roses are a good example. In the closed monastic society, which shut its members away from the world, gardens would have been an important contact with nature. Flowers brightened monastic as well as secular life. Gardens were often referred to as "paradise" in medieval literature, and paradise indeed they must have seemed to monks as they went about their various daily activities.

I n the arcades surrounding the cloister garth, the monks prayed, read, wrote, and washed. There are

vestiges of these pursuits in the Cuxa Cloister: a thirteenth-century Burgundian lavabo with two basins, one for washing hands and the other for cleaning Eucharistic vessels, and a twelfth-century lion's-head fountain from the monastery of Notre-Dame-du-Vilar, east of Cuxa, with a basin where the monks might have washed and filled buckets. (Monastic rules stated that the towels hung near a basin such as the last were for the monks to dry their hands and not to be used by the kitchen staff for drying greasy pots and pans.) Clothes were also washed and hung up to dry in cloisters.[30]

Lawns were often planted in cloister garths. Grass was just as troublesome during the Middle Ages as it is today, for it had to be weeded, mowed, and rolled. The complicated process of making a beautiful lawn for a pleasure garden was described by Albertus Magnus in the thirteenth century: first weeds were dug up by the roots and then

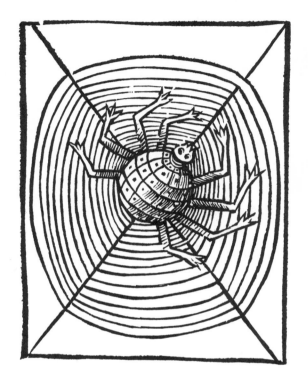

boiling water poured over the earth to kill any remaining roots and seeds. After that, turf was laid down and beaten with wooden mallets to compress the grass. The ideal lawn was level and thick.[31]

Albertus recommended planting trees around the lawn for shade, but he warned that they should not be planted in the middle of a lawn, where people were apt to walk, for "spiders' webs stretched from branch to branch would interrupt and entangle the faces of the passers-by."[32] In the Cuxa Cloister (where visitors do not walk on the lawns) there is a tree in each quadrant — a crab apple, a pear, a hawthorn, and a cornelian cherry.

In the Cuxa Cloister flowers line the interior edges of the lawns, providing a continuous array of color from early spring through late

fall. In March, when the cornelian cherry is covered with profuse yellow blossoms, crocus and spring snowflakes appear. In April and May the garden comes to life with jonquils, forget-me-nots, and Johnny-jump-ups. In late May and June the yellows, blues, and pinks of meadow rue, flax, columbine, and maiden pink carpet the garden. Foxglove and valerian follow. Later in June the pure-white Madonna lily, medieval symbol of purity, flowers on its tall stalk. All these plants were common in medieval Europe.

To ensure an effective display from spring to fall — a requirement that cannot be fulfilled by older plant species alone — some flowers that were not grown in the Middle Ages have been incorporated into the garden. These include candytuft, astilbe, bleeding-heart, sweet alyssum, coreopsis, balloon flower, coralbell, lobelia, *Torenia*, *Liriope*, anemone, and hybrid asters — all delicately colored flowers that blend with the subtle hues of the older varieties and are in character with a garden in a medieval setting. The choice of plants varies somewhat from year to year; the list that follows is not, therefore, definitive.

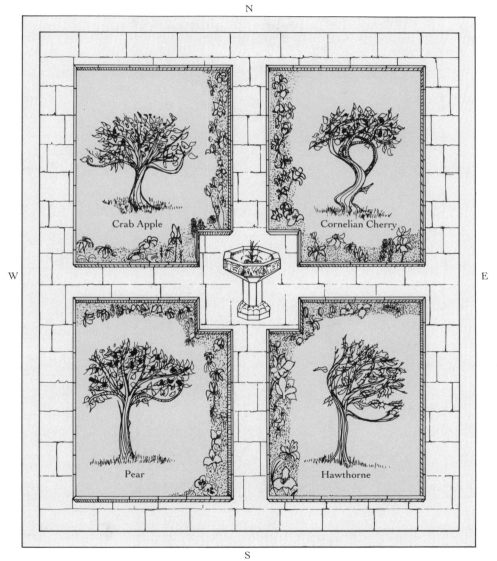

N

W

E

S

DIAGRAM OF THE CUXA CLOISTER GARTH GARDEN

PLANTS IN THE CUXA CLOISTER
GARTH GARDEN

°*Alchemilla vulgaris*	Lady's-Mantle
Allium neapolitanum	Flowering Onion
Anemone × *hybrida* 'Alba'	White Hybrid Anemone
°*Aquilegia vulgaris*	Columbine, European Crowfoot
Artemisia ludoviciana var. *albula*	Silver King Artemisia
Aster × *frikartii*	Hybrid Aster
Astilbe × *arendsii* 'Avalanche'	Astilbe
Campanula carpatica	Tussock, Bellflower
°*Campanula medium*	Canterbury-Bells
Campanula rotundifolia	Bluebell, Harebell
Chrysanthemum nipponicum	Nippon Chrysanthemum, Nippon Daisy
Coreopsis verticillata 'Golden Shower'	Threadleaf Coreopsis
°*Cornus mas*	Cornelian Cherry
°*Crataegus laevigata*	English Hawthorn
Crocus sieberi 'Firefly'	Crocus
Crocus sieberi 'Purpureus'	Crocus
Crocus sieberi 'Violet Queen'	Crocus
Dianthus deltoides	Maiden Pink
Dianthus gratianopolitanus	Cheddar Pink
Dicentra spectabilis	Bleeding-Heart
Digitalis purpurea 'Foxy'	Foxglove
Echinops ritro	Small Globe Thistle
Endymion hispanicus	Spanish Bluebell
°*Galanthus nivalis*	Common Snowdrop
Geranium endressii 'Wargrave Pink'	Pyrenean Cranesbill
°*Geranium sanguineum*	Cranesbill
Heuchera sanguinea	Coralbells
Iberis sempervirens	Candytuft
Iris reticulata 'Springtime'	Iris
Iris × 'Van Vliet'	Dutch Iris

°*Leucojum vernum*	Spring Snowflake
°*Lilium candidum*	Madonna Lily
Linum perenne	Perennial Flax
Liriope muscari 'Variegata'	Variegated Big Blue Lilyturf
Lobelia erinus	Lobelia
Lobularia maritima	Sweet Alyssum
Malus sargentii	Sargent Crab Apple
°*Muscari botryoides*	Common Grape Hyacinth
°*Myosotis scorpioides*	Forget-Me-Not
Narcissus cyclamineus 'Tête-à-Tête'	Narcissus
Narcissus jonquilla 'Simplex'	Jonquil
Narcissus 'Mt. Hood'	Daffodil, Trumpet Narcissus
°*Narcissus poeticus*	Pheasant's-Eye Narcissus, Poet's Narcissus
Narcissus triandrus 'Thalia'	Angel's-Tears
Nepeta mussinii	Catmint
Nierembergia hippomanica var. *violacea*	Blue Cupflower
Nierembergia scoparia	Tall Cupflower
Platycodon grandiflorus var. *mariesii*	Dwarf Balloon Flower
Platycodon grandiflorus var. *mariesii* 'Albus'	Dwarf White Balloon Flower
°*Polemonium caeruleum*	Jacob's-Ladder
°*Pyrus communis*	Pear
°*Ruta graveolens*	Rue, Herb-of-Grace
Salvia azurea var. *grandiflora*	Blue Sage
Scabiosa caucasica	Scabious, Pincushion Flower
Scilla siberica 'Spring Beauty'	Siberian Squill
Stachys byzantina	Woolly Betony, Lamb's-Ears
°*Stachys officinalis*	Betony
°*Thalictrum aquilegifolium*	Meadow Rue
Thalictrum speciosissimum	Meadow Rue
Torenia fournieri	Wishbone Flower

Trollius europaeus	Globeflower
°*Valeriana officinalis*	Common Valerian, Garden Heliotrope
Veronica prostrata 'Heavenly Blue'	Prostrate Speedwell
Veronica spicata 'Icicle'	Spiked Speedwell
°*Viola odorata*	Sweet Violet
°*Viola tricolor*	European Wild Pansy, Johnny-Jump-Up, Heartsease

The scientific and common names on this list follow, insofar as possible, L. H. Bailey, Hortus Third *and O. Polunin,* Flowers of Europe *(see Suggestions for Further Reading).*

°Medieval species

THE
BONNEFONT
CLOISTER
HERB GARDEN

Then my small patch was warmed
   by winds from the south
And the sun's heat. That it should
   not be washed away,
We faced it with planks and raised
   it in oblong beds
A little above the level ground.

Walahfrid Strabo,
ninth century[33]

A garden of herbs — plants used for cooking, medicines, and a variety of other practical purposes — was essential to every monastic community. Some monastic herb gardens, such as the twelfth-century garden at Christ Church, Canterbury, were within the main complex of the abbey, but utilitarian gardens were probably more often separate from the main cloistered areas. On the plan from St. Gall, for example, there are two herb gardens east of the church: a garden of medicinal herbs next to the physician's house, and a vegetable garden beside the gardener's house. The abbot of a monastery might also have had an herb garden, as did Walahfrid Strabo at Reichenau, and other important members of monastic communities often had their own gardens as well.

The herb garden in the Bonnefont Cloister is bordered on two sides by arcades with marble capitals from the late-thirteenth-century cloister of the Cistercian abbey at Bonnefont-en-Comminges and other monastic foundations in the Comminges region of southwestern France. Over two hundred and fifty species of plants that were used in the Middle Ages have been planted here. With the exception of the cloister arcades, the design of the garden gives an idea of how plants might have been

grown in secular as well as monastic herb gardens, but no attempt has been made to replicate any particular medieval garden. During the Middle Ages many of the plants — dandelion, mullein, celandine, and chicory, for example — might have been gathered in the wild rather than grown in gardens.

The plants in the Bonnefont garden (a diagram of this garden is shown on page 56) are labeled and grouped in nineteen beds, according to uses. The categories are not absolute, for in the Middle Ages most herbs served many purposes. The labels merely give the visitor some idea of the variety of ways in which herbs were employed in the medieval household. Horticultural considerations have also been taken into account; sun-loving plants are in the open, while those that grow better in the shade, such as ferns, aconite, sweet cicely, and wild ginger, are planted under the four quince trees at the center of the garden.

The beds are arranged symmetrically around a fifteenth-century Venetian wellhead. Although it does not now cover a well, the wellhead bears on its rim grooves left by ropes that drew buckets over its sides hundreds of years ago. A well, spring, pool, stream, or other water source was necessary for any medieval garden. At the Cistercian Abbey of Clairvaux, in the twelfth century, the garden was "divided into a number of beds by little canals which, though of still water, do flow slowly . . . the water thus serves a double purpose in sheltering the fish and irrigating the plants."[34] Walahfrid Strabo described the care with which he carried buckets of water to his thirsty plants and how he let the water drop slowly through

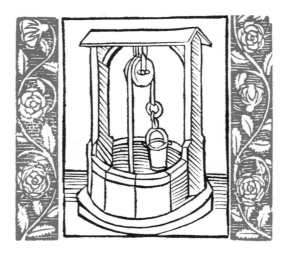

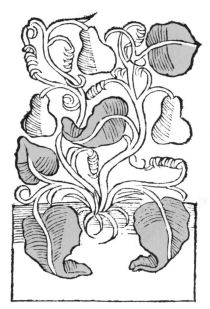

his fingers so it would not disturb the newly planted seeds. Watering pots with perforated spouts or holes in the bottom were also used. One fourteenth-century English gardener mentions an ingenious method of watering his gourds: ". . . so me thirl [I perforate] an earthen pot a small hole in the bottom and hang it full of water on a crooked stick with a feather in the hole that the water may [fall] thereon to water it."[35]

The quince in the beds at the center of the Bonnefont Cloister garden are examples of a type of fruit tree popular during the Middle Ages. They have delicate pink blossoms in the spring, and each fall their large golden fruits are the focal point of the garden. The other fruit trees in the Bonnefont garden are a cornelian cherry and an espaliered pear that grows against the wall of the Gothic chapel. The espaliered tree is the one feature of the garden that is not medieval, for the technique of training fruit trees in flat symmetrical patterns against vertical surfaces came into use later than the Middle Ages and is therefore not within the time period of The Cloisters. Nevertheless, this magnificent pear, planted in 1940, has become a permanent attraction at the Museum. The cornelian cherry is a species of dogwood; it gets its name from the edible red berries it bears in the fall, which look like cherries. Since monasteries were often surrounded by orchards, an orchard of crab apple trees has been planted outside the south wall of the Bonnefont garden.

The herbs in the Bonnefont garden are planted in beds filled with earth built up several inches above the level of the paths. Brick edging holds the soil in place. This gardening technique was common in northern Europe throughout the Middle Ages. Walahfrid Strabo used it, and numerous medieval manuscript paintings show garden plots laid out in symmetrically arranged square or rectangular raised beds edged with bricks or wooden planks. Functional, neat, and easy to care for, gardens with raised beds are becoming popular again today. Since the beds can be raised to any height, they have the added advantage of making gardening possible for people who cannot bend — the elderly and those in wheelchairs, for example.

The four central beds are bordered by wattle, medieval fences constructed of flexible branches woven through upright stakes. A wattle fence is depicted on a small sixteenth-century ivory pedestal exhibited in the Glass Gallery, next to the Bonnefont Cloister. Wattle was also used to brace the sides of garden seats made of mounded turf, as shown in a fifteenth-century stained glass roundel depicting a game of quintain in the Glass Gallery.

Next to the wall of the Gothic Chapel, at the northwest corner of the garden, is a garden house in which tools are stored. Most of these tools — shovels, spades, rakes, ladders, baskets, hammers, pruning saws, and the like — are not very different from those used by medieval gardeners. Few medieval gardening implements survive, but they are often depicted in manuscript illustrations. The illustration on page 5, for example, from an early-sixteenth-century German edition of *Opus ruralium commodorum* by Petrus de Crescentiis, shows a gardener who carries a wicker basket, perhaps with dung for manure. A sharp knife hangs from his belt, and at his feet is his wooden shovel with an iron "shoe" riveted to its rim. Metal was expensive and used only

on the cutting edges of shovels. The illustration below depicts a gardener planting leeks. He has hacked out the trenches with a mattock, a digging tool whose blade is set at right angles to its handle. Walahfrid Strabo called the mattock the "tooth of Saturn" and used it to attack the tough nettles that invaded his garden.

The garden house in the Bonnefont Cloister garden is also used for drying sage, thyme, marjoram, tansy, lavender, sorrel, mint, sneezewort, yarrow, savory, hyssop and other herbs from the garden. These are hung upside down in bunches, filling the shed with their fragrance. During the Middle Ages, herbs like these were used for cooking, medicines, dyes, insecticides, and cosmetics. At The Cloisters they are made into bouquets that add color and fragrance to the Museum during the winter months.

The Bonnefont Cloister contains only species of plants known in the Middle Ages. The list that follows is not intended to include all medieval plants; it is, rather, a list of plants suitable for this particular garden at The Cloisters. The choice is limited by the amount of space available, as well as by climatic considerations. Not all the plants on the list will be found in the garden in any one year; the selection depends on the availability of seeds. It should be remembered that during the Middle Ages some of these plants would have been found in the wild rather than cultivated in gardens.

In several instances the name of a plant is followed by another name in parentheses. This second name is of a species grown as a substitute for a medieval species that is unobtainable.

Controversy exists concerning the exact identification of some plants that are mentioned in medieval literature and depicted in medieval art. It is often extremely difficult to identify plants from the names given them by medieval writers, while plants in works of art are not always rendered with botanical accuracy. The list presented here is drawn from many sources, including the list of plants of the Middle Ages in John Harvey, *Medieval Gardens* (see Suggestions for Further Reading), and the list of medieval plants in Hermann Fischer, *Mittelalterliche Pflanzenkunde* (1929. Reprint. Hildesheim: Olms, 1967). In many cases we have called upon the expertise of Frank Anderson, honorary curator of Rare Books and Manuscripts at the New York Botanical Garden, and have benefited from his extensive knowledge of plants mentioned in medieval herbals. The list will be amended and changed as new research on the plants of the Middle Ages becomes available.

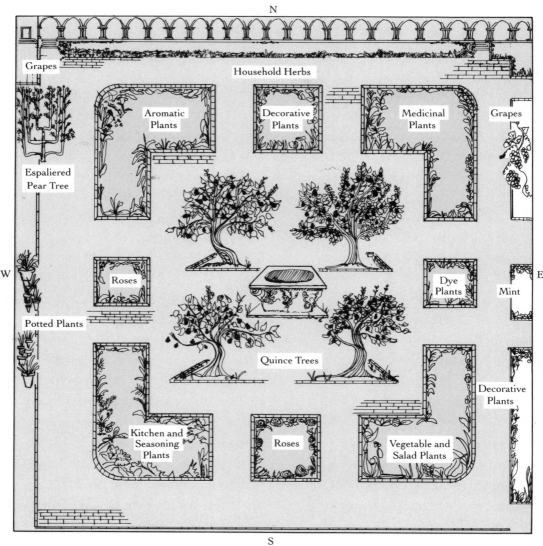

N

Grapes

Household Herbs

Aromatic
Plants

Decorative
Plants

Medicinal
Plants

Grapes

Espaliered
Pear Tree

W

Roses

Dye
Plants

E

Mint

Potted Plants

Quince Trees

Decorative
Plants

Kitchen and
Seasoning
Plants

Roses

Vegetable and
Salad Plants

S

DIAGRAM OF THE BONNEFONT CLOISTER HERB GARDEN

PLANTS IN THE
BONNEFONT CLOISTER
HERB GARDEN

Achillea millefolium	Common Yarrow, Milfoil
Achillea ptarmica	Sneezewort, Sneezeweed
Aconitum napellus	Monkshood, Aconite, Garden Wolfsbane
Acorus calamus	Sweet Flag, Calamus
Adonis aestivalis	Pheasant's-Eye, Summer Adonis
Agrimonia eupatoria	Agrimony
Agrostemma githago	Corn Cockle
Ajuga reptans	Bugle
Alcea rosea	Hollyhock
Alchemilla vulgaris	Lady's-Mantle
Alkanna tinctoria	Dyer's Alkanet
Allium cepa [Aggregatum Group]	Shallot
Allium cepa	Onion
Allium ampeloprasum [Porrum Group]	Leek
Allium sativum	Garlic
Allium schoenoprasum	Chive
Allium ursinum	Ramsons, Bear's Garlic
Althaea officinalis	Marsh Mallow
Anagallis arvensis	Scarlet Pimpernel
Anagallis arvensis caerulea	Blue Pimpernel
Anchusa officinalis	Bugloss, Alkanet
Anemone coronaria	Crown Anemone, Poppy Anemone
Anemone pulsatilla	Pasque Flower
Anethum graveolens	Dill
Angelica archangelica	Angelica
Anthemis tinctoria	Golden Marguerite
Anthriscus cerefolium	Chervil
Antirrhinum majus	Common Snapdragon
Apium graveolens	Wild Celery
Aquilegia vulgaris	Columbine, European Crowfoot

Aristolochia clematitis	Birthwort
Armeria maritima	Thrift, Sea Pink
Armoracia rusticana	Horseradish
Artemisia abrotanum	Southernwood
Artemisia absinthium	Absinthe, Wormwood
Artemisia camphorata	Camphor Artemisia
Artemisia dracunculus	Tarragon, Estragon
Artemisia vulgaris	Mugwort
Arum italicum	Italian Arum
Arum maculatum	Cuckoopint, Lords-and-Ladies
Asarum europaeum	Asarabacca, European Wild Ginger
Asparagus officinalis	Asparagus
Atriplex hortensis	Orach
Atropa belladonna	Deadly Nightshade, Belladonna
Bellis perennis	English Daisy
Beta vulgaris	Beet
Borago officinalis	Borage
Botrychium lunaria	Moonwort, Grape Fern
Brassica nigra	Black Mustard
Bryonia dioica	Red Bryony
Buxus sempervirens	Boxwood
Calendula officinalis	Pot Marigold
Campanula medium	Canterbury-Bells
Campanula rapunculus	Rampion
Carlina acaulis	Carline Thistle
Carthamus tinctorius	Safflower, False Saffron
Carum carvi	Caraway
Catananche caerulea	Cupid's-Dart, Cupidone
Centaurea cyanus	Cornflower, Bachelor's-Button, Bluebottle
Chamaemelum nobile	Chamomile

Cheiranthus cheiri	Wallflower
Chelidonium majus	Greater Celandine
Chenopodium bonus-henricus	Good-King-Henry
Chenopodium botrys	Jerusalem Oak
Chrysanthemum balsamita	Alecost, Costmary
Chrysanthemum cinerariifolium	Pyrethrum
Chrysanthemum leucanthemum	Marguerite, Oxeye Daisy
Chrysanthemum parthenium	Feverfew
Chrysanthemum segetum	Corn Marigold
Cichorium endivia	Endive
Cichorium intybus	Chicory
Cnicus benedictus	Blessed Thistle
Colchicum autumnale	Meadow Saffron, Naked Ladies, Autumn Crocus
Consolida regalis	Larkspur
Convallaria majalis	Lily-of-the-Valley
Coriandrum sativum	Coriander
Cornus mas	Cornelian Cherry
Crithmum maritimum	Samphire
Crocus sativus	Saffron Crocus
Cucubalus baccifer	Berry Catchfly
Cuminum cyminum	Cumin
Cydonia oblonga	Quince
Cytisus scoparius	Scotch Broom
Daphne cneorum	Garland Flower
Daphne mezereum	February Daphne, Mezereon
Datura stramonium	Jimsonweed, Thorn Apple
Daucus carota	Wild Carrot, Queen-Anne's-Lace
Delphinium staphisagria	Stavesacre
Dianthus barbatus	Sweet William
Dianthus carthusianorum	Cluster-Head Pink

Dianthus caryophyllus	Clove Pink, Carnation
Dictamnus albus	Dittany, Fraxinella, Gas Plant
Digitalis purpurea	Foxglove
Dipsacus sativus	Fuller's Teasel
Dryopteris filix-mas	Male Fern
Endymion non-scriptus	English Bluebell
Eruca vesicaria subsp. *sativa*	Rocket
Eryngium maritimum (here *E. planum*)	Sea Holly, Eryngo
Euphorbia lathyris	Caper Spurge, Mole Plant
Filipendula ulmaria	Meadowsweet, Queen-of-the-Meadow
Foeniculum vulgare	Fennel
Fragaria vesca	Wild Strawberry
Galega officinalis	Goat's Rue
Galium odoratum	Sweet Woodruff
Galium verum	Our-Lady's Bedstraw
Genista tinctoria	Dyer's Greenweed
Gentiana lutea	Yellow Gentian
Geranium robertianum	Herb Robert, Red Robin
Geranium sanguineum	Cranesbill
Geum rivale	Avens, Water Avens
Geum urbanum	Cloveroot, Herb Bennet
Glechoma hederacea	Ground Ivy, Alehoof, Gill-over-the-Ground
Glycyrrhiza glabra	Liquorice
Helleborus foetidus	Bear's Foot, Stinking Hellebore
Helleborus niger	Christmas Rose
Helleborus orientalis	Lenten Rose
Hesperis matronalis	Dame's Rocket, Sweet Rocket
Humulus lupulus	Hop
Hyoscyamus niger	Henbane
Hypericum perforatum	St.-John's-Wort

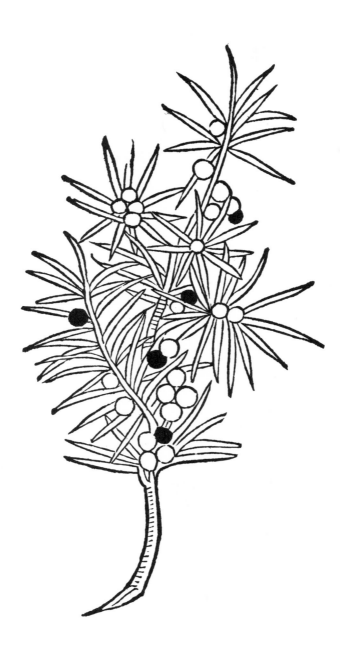

Hyssopus officinalis	Hyssop
Inula helenium	Elecampane
Iris foetidissima	Gladwin, Stinking Iris
Iris × germanica (here *I.* 'Lavanesque')	Flag, Fleur-de-Lis
Iris × germanica var. *florentina*	Orris
Iris pallida	Pale Iris, Orris
Iris pseudacorus	Yellow Flag
Isatis tinctoria	Woad
Juniperus communis	Common Juniper
Juniperus sabina	Savin
Lamium maculatum	Spotted Dead Nettle
Laurus nobilis	Laurel, Bay, Sweet Bay
Lavandula angustifolia subsp. *angustifolia*	Lavender
Lavandula stoechas	French Lavender
Leontopodium alpinum	Edelweiss
Leonurus cardiaca	Motherwort
Leucojum vernum	Spring Snowflake
Levisticum officinale	Lovage
Lilium candidum	Madonna Lily
Linaria vulgaris	Toadflax, Butter-and-Eggs
Linum usitatissimum	Flax
Lonicera periclymenum	Honeysuckle, Woodbine
Lunaria annua	Honesty, Silver-Dollar
Lychnis coronaria	Rose Campion, Mullein Pink
Lychnis flos-cuculi	Cuckoo Flower, Ragged-Robin
Lysimachia vulgaris	Yellow Loosestrife
Malva alcea (here *M. alcea* var. *fastigiata*)	Mallow
Malva sylvestris	High Mallow, Cheeses
Mandragora officinarum	Mandrake
Marrubium vulgare	Horehound

Matricaria recutita	Wild Chamomile, Sweet False Chamomile
Matthiola incana	Stock, Gillyflower
Matthiola longipetala subsp. *bicornis*	Evening Stock
Melilotus officinalis	Melilot, Sweet Clover
Melissa officinalis	Lemon Balm
Mentha aquatica	Water Mint
Mentha longifolia	Horsemint
Mentha × piperita	Peppermint
Mentha pulegium	Pennyroyal
Mentha spicata	Spearmint
Mentha suaveolens	Apple Mint
Mercurialis annua	Annual Mercury
Muscari botryoides	Common Grape Hyacinth
Myosotis scorpioides	Forget-Me-Not
Myrrhis odorata	Sweet Cicely, Myrrh
Narcissus jonquilla	Jonquil
Narcissus poeticus	Pheasant's-Eye, Poet's Narcissus
Narcissus pseudonarcissus	Daffodil, Trumpet Narcissus
Nepeta cataria	Catnip
Nigella arvensis	Wild Fennel
Nigella damascena	Love-in-a-Mist
Nigella sativa	Black Cumin
Ocimum basilicum	Sweet Basil
Ocimum basilicum 'Minimum'	Small-leaved Basil
Onopordum acanthium	Cotton Thistle, Scotch Thistle
Origanum dictamnus	Dittany of Crete
Origanum majorana	Sweet Marjoram
Origanum vulgare	Wild Marjoram, Pot Marjoram
Ornithogalum umbellatum	Star-of-Bethlehem
Osmunda regalis	Royal Fern

Paeonia officinalis	Peony
Papaver rhoeas	Corn Poppy, Field Poppy
Pastinaca sativa	Parsnip
Petroselinum crispum	Parsley
Phyllitis scolopendrium	Hart's-Tongue Fern
Physalis alkekengi	Chinese-Lantern, Winter Cherry
Pimpinella anisum	Common Anise
Plantago major	Common Plantain
Polemonium caeruleum	Jacob's-Ladder
Polygonum bistorta	Bistort
Polypodium vulgare	European Polypody, Wall Fern
Potentilla reptans	Cinquefoil
Poterium sanguisorba	Salad Burnet
Primula auricula	Auricula, Bear's-Ear
Primula elatior	Oxlip
Primula veris	Cowslip
Primula vulgaris	English Primrose
Pulmonaria officinalis	Lungwort
Pyrus communis	Pear
Raphanus sativus	Radish
Reseda luteola	Dyer's Rocket, Weld
Rosa × *alba* (here *R.* × *alba* 'Suaveolens')	White Rose
Rosa canina	Dog Rose
Rosa centifolia 'Blanche Moreau'	Cabbage Rose
Rosa centifolia 'Muscosa'	Moss Rose
Rosa damascena 'Trigintipetala'	Damask Rose
Rosa eglanteria	Sweetbriar, Eglantine
Rosa gallica	French Rose
Rosa gallica var. *officinalis*	Apothecary Rose
Rosa gallica var. *versicolor*	Rosa Mundi

Rosa villosa	Apple Rose
Rosmarinus officinalis	Rosemary
Rubia tinctorum	Madder
Rumex acetosa	Garden Sorrel
Rumex scutatus	French Sorrel
Ruscus aculeatus	Butcher's-Broom
Ruta graveolens	Rue, Herb-of-Grace
Salvia officinalis	Sage
Salvia pratensis	Meadow Clary
Salvia sclarea	Clary
Santolina chamaecyparissus	Lavender Cotton
Saponaria officinalis	Soapwort, Bouncing Bet
Satureja hortensis	Summer Savory
Satureja montana	Winter Savory
Scrophularia nodosa	Figwort, Throatwort
Sedum acre	Stonecrop, Wall-Pepper
Sedum album	White Stonecrop
Sedum telephium	Orpine, Live-Forever
Sempervivum tectorum	Common Houseleek, Hen-and-Chickens
Senecio doronicum	Leopard's-Bane
Silene alba	White Campion, Evening Campion, White Cockle
Silybum marianum	St. Mary's Thistle, Milk Thistle
Sium sisarum	Skirret
Stachys officinalis	Betony
Symphytum officinale	Comfrey, Boneset
Tanacetum vulgare	Common Tansy
Taraxacum officinale	Dandelion
Teucrium chamaedrys	Germander
Thalictrum aquilegifolium	Meadow Rue
Thymus serpyllum	Wild Thyme

Thymus vulgaris	Common Thyme
Trigonella foenum-graecum	Fenugreek
Valeriana officinalis	Common Valerian, Garden Heliotrope
Veratrum album	European White Hellebore
Verbascum thapsus	Common Mullein
Verbena officinalis	Vervain
Vinca minor	Common Periwinkle, Myrtle
Viola canina	Dog Violet
Viola odorata	Sweet Violet
Viola tricolor	European Wild Pansy, Johnny-Jump-Up, Heartsease
Vitex agnus-castus	Chaste Tree
Vitis vinifera	Grape

The scientific and common names on this list follow, insofar as possible, L. H. Bailey, Hortus Third *and O. Polunin,* Flowers of Europe *(see Suggestions for Further Reading).*

THE
TRIE CLOISTER
GARDEN

Unicornis the Unicorn, which is also called Rhinoceros by the Greeks, is of the following nature. He is a very small animal like a kid, excessively swift, with one horn in the middle of his forehead, and no hunter can catch him. But he can be trapped by the following stratagem.

A virgin girl is led to where he lurks, and there she is sent off by herself into the wood. He soon leaps into her lap when he sees her, and embraces her, and hence he gets caught.

Latin bestiary,
twelfth century[36]

Unlike the Bonnefont Cloister garden, the garden in the Trie Cloister has no precedent in medieval horticulture. This unique garden consists of plants depicted in the Hunt of the Unicorn, a series of seven tapestries belonging to the Museum. The tapestries, woven around 1500, tell the story of the pursuit and slaying of the unicorn, an imaginary beast with a single horn who could only be captured by a virgin. The first tapestry portrays the start of the chase, as the hunters enter a forest in search of their prey. In the succeeding tapestries the unicorn is seen purifying the waters of a stream, leaping the stream, defending himself against the hunters and their dogs, surrendering to the maiden, and being killed and delivered to a lord and lady of a castle. In the seventh tapestry he is alive again, a symbol of the resur-

rected Christ, resting under a pomegranate tree. This and all the other scenes are laden with Christian as well as secular symbolism.

All the tapestries are rich in flowers, shrubs, and trees. The first and seventh in the series are properly called *millefleurs* tapestries, for in them the action takes place against flat, carpet-like backgrounds of daffodils, wild strawberries, English daisies, thistles, pinks, wallflowers, sweet violets, periwinkle, primroses, English bluebells, and other flowers. There is no illusion of depth. Some attempt is made to represent the third dimension in the other five tapestries, for the plants are depicted as if growing naturally along the bank of a stream, in dense clusters of bushes and trees that recede into the depths of the forest,

or, in the scene in which the unicorn surrenders to the maiden, against a wooden fence.

About 85 percent of the more than one hundred species of plants depicted in the tapestries have been identified. Many are easy to recognize — Madonna lily, wild strawberry, sweet violet, carnation, and rose are a few examples — but some of the plants cannot be classified botanically.

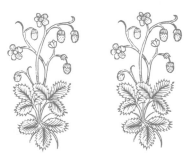

Chemical analysis has shown that all of the many colors in the tapestries were produced from combinations of dyes made from only three plants: madder, whose roots yield a red; woad, from whose leaves a blue is extracted; and weld, whose leaves, stems, and seeds give yellow. Madder, woad, and weld grow in the Bonnefont Cloister herb garden.

About fifty species of flora depicted in the Unicorn tapestries have been planted in the Trie Cloister garden. This garden is enclosed by arcades incorporating late-fifteenth-century marble capitals and bases from the Carmelite convent at Trie-en-Bigorre and other monasteries in the Bigorre region of southwestern France. Space and horticultural limitations make it impossible to include all of the identifiable plants depicted in the tapestries. As in the tapestries, however, the garden is conceived as an impenetrable mass of flowers, trees, and shrubs, without paths or openings. Although it includes flora from all seven tapestries, in design the garden most closely resembles the second tapestry in the series, which depicts the unicorn at the fountain. In that scene the hunters have discovered the unicorn kneeling to dip his horn into a stream that he cleanses of poisons. The Trie Cloister garden is also dominated by a large central

fountain, and many of the plants are arranged as in the tapestry, with sage and a rosebush growing at the base of the fountain, white campion, Johnny-jump-ups, pot marigolds, carnations, and an orange tree placed toward the front, and an oak among the several trees toward the back. The blackberry bush entwined in the branches of a hazelnut tree on the east side of the garden is reminiscent of a detail of the sixth tapestry.

Although the Trie Cloister garden is inspired by the plants, designs, colors, and textures of the Unicorn Tapestries, it cannot duplicate one aspect of the works of art — the fact that in the tapestries all the plants, whether spring, summer, or fall blooming, are simultaneously in full flower and fruit. In the real garden, each plant must bloom in its proper season. The first spring flowers are English bluebells and daffodils, followed by Johnny-jump-ups, sweet violets, English daisies, forget-me-nots, primroses, and wallflowers in late April and May. In June the garden is bright with the flowers of columbine, oxeye daisies, clary, bistort, flag, feverfew, clove pink, Madonna lily, and cabbage rose. Throughout the summer, daylilies, milk thistles, pot marigolds, corn marigolds, and wild strawberries add splashes of color as they come into bloom and fruit, and in the fall brilliant orange Chinese-lantern pods predominate. All the flowers stand out against a leafy backdrop of periwinkle, lady's-mantle, and sweet violet.

Of the twenty species of trees pictured in the tapestries, seven — medlar, linden, hazelnut, English oak, holly, pomegranate, and orange — grow in the garden. (These trees are indicated on the diagram of the garden, page 76.) The last two, subtropical plants that cannot survive northern winters, are taken indoors in October. All the other plants in the garden were common, either cultivated or growing in the wild, in northern Europe during the Middle Ages.

All the plants on the Trie Cloister list have been identified in the Unicorn Tapestries. The main source here is the 1941 work by Alexander and Woodward, *The Flora of the Unicorn Tapestries* (see Suggestions for Further Reading). Alexander and Woodward identified about 83 species in the seven tapestries. Be-

cause of space limitations only 54 of these have been included in the Trie Cloister garden.

The Alexander and Woodward publication is the most important work on the flora of the Unicorn Tapestries to date, but the authors were not able to identify all the plants, and some of their identifications are questionable. At this time the Trie Cloister garden includes a number of plants whose identities in the tapestries are not certain. Research continues on the plants of the Unicorn Tapestries, and this list will no doubt be altered in the future.

As with the Bonnefont garden list, not all the plants on the Trie Cloister list will be found in the garden in any one year.

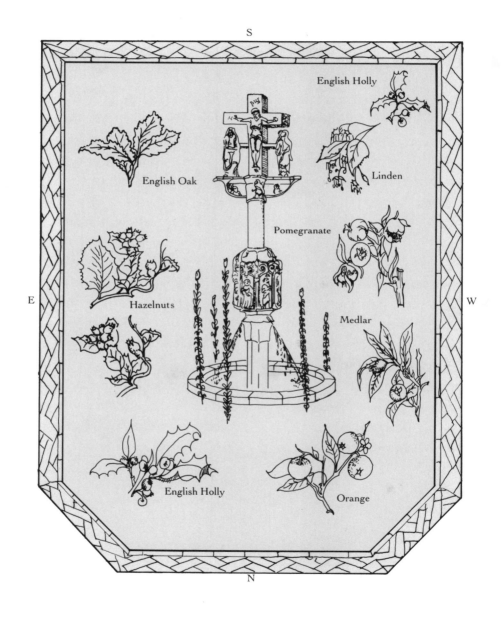

S

English Holly

English Oak

Linden

Pomegranate

E   W

Hazelnuts

Medlar

English Holly

Orange

N

DIAGRAM OF THE TRIE CLOISTER GARDEN

PLANTS IN THE
TRIE CLOISTER GARDEN

Alchemilla vulgaris	Lady's-Mantle
Aquilegia vulgaris	Columbine, European Crowfoot
Arum maculatum	Cuckoopint, Lords-and-Ladies
Bellis perennis	English Daisy
Calendula officinalis	Pot Marigold
Carthamus tinctorius	Safflower, False Saffron
Centaurea cyanus	Cornflower, Bachelor's-Button, Bluebottle
Cheiranthus cheiri	Wallflower
Chrysanthemum leucanthemum	Marguerite, Oxeye Daisy
Chrysanthemum parthenium	Feverfew
Chrysanthemum segetum	Corn Marigold
Citrus aurantium	Seville Orange, Sour Orange
Corylus avellana	European Hazelnut, European Filbert
Cucubalus baccifer	Berry Catchfly
Dianthus caryophyllus	Clove Pink, Carnation
Endymion non-scriptus	English Bluebell
Fragaria vesca	Wild Strawberry
Hemerocallis fulva	Orange Daylily
Hesperis matronalis	Dame's Rocket, Sweet Rocket
Hieracium sp.	Hawkweed
Ilex aquifolium	English Holly, European Holly
Inula sp.	Elecampane
Iris × *germanica*	Flag, Fleur-de-Lis
Lilium candidum	Madonna Lily
Lunaria annua	Honesty, Silver-Dollar
Matthiola incana	Stock, Gillyflower
Mespilus germanica	Medlar
Myosotis scorpioides	Forget-Me-Not
Narcissus pseudonarcissus	Daffodil, Trumpet Narcissus
Nigella arvensis	Wild Fennel

Orchis mascula	Early Purple Orchid
Phyllitis scolopendrium	Hart's-Tongue Fern
Physalis alkekengi	Chinese-Lantern, Winter Cherry
Plantago major	Common Plantain
Polygonum bistorta	Bistort
Primula elatior	Oxlip
Primula vulgaris	English Primrose
Punica granatum	Pomegranate
Quercus robur	English Oak
Rosa centifolia	Cabbage Rose
Rubus fruticosus	Blackberry
Rumex acetosa	Garden Sorrel
Ruscus aculeatus	Butcher's-Broom
Salvia officinalis	Sage
Salvia sclarea	Clary
Senecio doronicum	Leopard's-Bane
Silene alba	White Campion, Evening Campion, White Cockle
Silybum marianum	St. Mary's Thistle, Milk Thistle
Taraxacum officinale	Dandelion
Tilia × europaea	Linden
Vinca minor	Common Periwinkle, Myrtle
Viola canina	Dog Violet
Viola odorata	Sweet Violet
Viola tricolor	European Wild Pansy, Johnny-Jump-Up, Heartsease

The scientific and common names on this list follow, insofar as possible, L. H. Bailey, Hortus Third *and O. Polunin,* Flowers of Europe *(see Suggestions for Further Reading).*

INDOOR PLANTS: THE SAINT-GUILHEM AND CUXA CLOISTERS

Violets and gilliflowers. . . . when the frosts draw near, you should replant in pots, at a season when the moon waneth, in order to set them under cover and keep them from the cold in a cellar, and by day set them in the air or in the sun and water them at such time that the water may be drunken up and the earth dry before you set them under cover, for never should you put them away wet in the evening.

The Goodman of Paris,
fourteenth century[37]

We know that medieval people kept plants in containers as well as in gardens, for potted plants and window boxes are depicted in medieval manuscript paintings. The illustration on page 82, from a sixteenth-century German edition of *Opus ruralium commodorum* by Petrus de Crescentiis, shows a woman watering a rosemary tree that grows in a wooden tub. The container is very much like those used for oleander and citrus trees at The Cloisters.

In the passage quoted at the opening of this chapter, the Goodman of Paris instructed his wife on transplanting violets and gillyflowers into pots and on bringing them indoors for the winter. There may even be medieval precedents for the use of cloisters as winter conservatories, if one believes a fourteenth-century account that Albertus Magnus amazed visitors to his cloister in Cologne by showing them flowering plants and ripe fruit on his trees in January.[38]

From October through April the arcades of the Cuxa Cloister are covered with plate-glass panels to conserve heat, and the cloister becomes a winter conservatory. Potted plants — citrus, acanthus, carob, palm, jasmine, aloe, myrtle, rosemary, and bay — and the forced flowers of narcissus, grape hyacinth, freesias, lily-of-the-valley, crocus, and Madonna lily transform the interior of the cloister into a fragrant indoor garden.

A small garden is maintained throughout the winter months in the Saint-Guilhem Cloister, which is entirely indoors and covered by a skylight. From Christmas through Easter a raised bed around the central fountain (a converted eleventh-century column capital) is planted with flowering bulbs, ivy, and ferns, giving this cloister the appearance of spring even when the outdoor gardens are covered with snow.

Flowers and herbs from the gardens of The Cloisters brighten many rooms in the Museum all year round. As often as they come into bloom, Madonna lilies are placed in a fifteenth-century glazed earthenware vase near the Mérode altarpiece, where they echo the Madonna lily on the table in the center of the painting. Throughout the summer months vases of fresh flowers adorn the main hall. These arrangements are varied and unusual — for example,

combinations of hyssop, lady's-mantle, and feverfew; or hesperis, white campion, and wild strawberries. During the winter there are bouquets of dried flowers, and for Christmas the main hall is decorated with an eight-foot wreath of dried herbs — artemisia, tansy, Chinese-lantern, royal fern, lady's-mantle, honesty, betony, sage, lavender, love-in-a-mist, rosemary, and other plants that grow in the gardens of The Cloisters. Container plants in summer are found outside in the Bonnefont Garden and on the West Terrace and in winter in the arcades of the Cuxa Cloister.

PLANTS IN CONTAINERS

Acanthus mollis	Artist's Acanthus, Bear's-Breech
Aloe barbadensis	Medicinal Aloe
Ceratonia siliqua	Carob, St. John's-Bread
Citrus aurantium	Seville Orange, Sour Orange
Ficus carica	Common Fig
Jasminum officinale	Poet's Jessamine
Laurus nobilis	Laurel, Bay, Sweet Bay
Myrtus communis	Myrtle
Nerium oleander	Common Oleander
Olea europaea	Common Olive
Phoenix dactylifera (here *P. roebelenii*)	Date Palm
Punica granatum (here *P. granatum* 'Nana')	Pomegranate
Rosmarinus officinalis	Rosemary
Urginea maritima	Sea Onion, Squill

The scientific and common names on this list follow, insofar as possible, L. H. Bailey, Hortus Third *and* O. Polunin, Flowers of Europe *(see Suggestions for Further Reading).*

NOTES

The quotation on p. v is from *Medieval and Renaissance Poets*, edited by E. Talbot Donaldson (New York: Viking, 1950), p. 50.

1. Helen Waddell, *Mediaeval Latin Lyrics*, 4th rev. ed. (1933. Reprint. London: Penguin Books, 1968), p. 107.

2. Walahfrid Strabo, *Hortulus*, translated by Raef Payne, with commentary by Wilfrid Blunt (Pittsburgh: The Hunt Botanical Library, 1966), p. 25.

3. *Butler's Lives of the Saints*, edited by Herbert Thurston, S.J., and Donald Attwater, 4 vols. (New York: P.J. Kennedy & Sons, 1963), vol. 4, p. 164.

4. *St. Benedict's Rule for Monasteries*, translated by Leonard J. Doyle (Collegeville, Minnesota: The Liturgical Press, 1948), p. 94.

5. *Capitulare de villis vel curtis imperialibus (Directives for the Administration of Imperial Courts or Estates)*, translated by John Asch in *Garden Journal*, vol. 18, no. 5 (September/October, 1968), pp. 134–147.

6. Giovanni Boccaccio, *The Decameron*, translated by Richard Aldington (Garden City, New York: Garden City Publishing Company, 1930), pp. 135–136.

7. All the quotations in this paragraph are from John Harvey, *Medieval Gardens* (Beaverton, Oregon: Timber Press, 1981), p. 6.

8. To date there is no modern edition of Petrus de Crescentiis's treatise, *Opus ruralium commodorum*. English translations of sections of the work can be found in Frank Crisp, *Medieval Gardens*, 2d ed. (New York: Hacker, 1972), Eleanour Sinclair Rohde, *The Story of the Garden* (Boston: Hale, Cushman & Flint, 1936), and elsewhere. For good discussions of this work see Frank Anderson, *An Illustrated History of the Herbals* (New York: Columbia University Press, 1977), and John Harvey, *Medieval Gardens*.

9. *The Goodman of Paris*, translated and introduced by Eileen Power (London: Routledge, 1928).

10. Ibid., Introduction, pp. 23–24.

11. Eleanour Sinclair Rohde, *A Garden of Herbs*, rev. ed. (New York: Dover, 1969), p. 134.

12. Ibid., p. 165.

13. The references are from *Herbarium: Natural Remedies from a Medieval Manuscript*, with texts by Adalberto Pazzini and

Emma Pirani (New York: Rizzoli, 1980), which is based on a fourteenth-century illustrated edition of the *Tacuinum* known as the *Theatrum sanitatis.*

14. *Banckes's Herbal,* an anonymous work printed by Richard Banckes in London in 1525, has been edited and transcribed into modern English by Sanford V. Larkey and Thomas Pyles, *An Herbal [1525]* (New York: New York Botanical Garden), 1941.

15. This was prescribed by the twelfth-century abbess and mystic, Hildegard of Bingen. Monks and nuns cared for the sick in their abbeys and convents. Hildegard's book, *Physica,* which includes discussions of the medicinal uses of hundreds of plants, is a compilation of her knowledge of natural science. The book has been translated into German by Peter Riethe as *Naturkunde,* 2d ed. (Salzburg: Otto Müller, 1974).

16. Pazzini and Pirani, *Herbarium.*

17. Ibid.

18. Margaret B. Freeman, *Herbs for the Mediaeval Household* (New York: The Metropolitan Museum of Art, 1979), p. 29.

19. The Goodman of Paris recommended the following for killing wolves and foxes: "Take the root of black hellebore (it is the hellebore that hath a white flower) and dry the root thoroughly and not in the sun, and clean the earth therefrom; and then make it into powder in a mortar and with this powder mix a fifth part of glass well ground and a fourth part of lily leaf, and let it all be mixed and pounded together, so that it can be passed through a sieve . . . take honey and fresh fat in equal part and mix them with the aforesaid powder, and make it into a hard and stiff paste, rolling it into round balls of the size of a hen's egg, and cover the aforesaid balls with fresh fat and lay them upon stones and shards, in the places where . . . wolves and foxes will come." Rats could be killed, according to the Goodman, by "making cakes of paste and toasted cheese and powdered aconite and setting these near to their holes, where they have naught to drink." Power, *The Goodman of Paris,* pp. 212–213.

20. Teresa McLean, *Medieval English Gardens* (New York: Viking, 1980), pp. 69, 158.

21. The uses of plants in medieval painting are discussed by Daniel V. Thompson, *The Materials and Techniques of Medieval Painting* (1936. Reprint. New York: Dover, 1956).

22. Freeman, *Herbs for the Mediaeval Household*, p. x.

23. Pazzini and Pirani, *Herbarium*.

24. Riethe, *Naturkunde*, p. 76.

25. Rohde, *The Story of the Garden*, p. 44.

26. *The Greek Herbal of Dioscorides*, edited by Robert T. Gunther (London and New York: Hafner, 1968).

27. Emile Mâle, *The Gothic Image*, translated by Dora Nussey (New York: Harper Torchbooks, 1958), pp. 51–52.

28. Marie Luise Gothein, *A History of Garden Art*, translated by Mrs. Archer-Hind, 2 vols. (London: Dent; New York: Dutton, 1928), vol. 1, p. 174.

29. See John Harvey's review of Marilyn Stokstad and Jerry Stannard, *Gardens of the Middle Ages*, in *Garden History* 11 (1983): 177.

30. For these and other details of daily life in monastic cloisters, see Paul Meyvaert, "The Medieval Monastic Claustrum," *Gesta* 12 (1973): 55–56.

31. Harvey, *Medieval Gardens*, p. 6.

32. Ibid.

33. Walahfrid Strabo, *Hortulus*, p. 29.

34. Harvey, *Medieval Gardens*, p. 8.

35. Ibid., p. 160. The Goodman of Paris watered his pumpkins this way: "and keep the stem ever moist, by hanging a pot with a hole therein on a stick, and in the pot a straw and some water, etc., or a strip of new cloth." Power, *The Goodman of Paris*, p. 198.

36. T. H. White, *The Bestiary* (New York: Putnam, 1960), pp. 20–21.

37. Power, *The Goodman of Paris*, p. 197. The gilliflowers referred to here were clove-pink carnations (*Dianthus caryophyllus*), which were used in cooking for their clove-like flavor. See McLean, *Medieval English Gardens*, pp. 150–151.

38. Harvey, *Medieval Gardens*, p. 75, and Gothein, *A History of Garden Art*, p. 196.

SUGGESTIONS FOR FURTHER READING

Alexander, E.J., and Carol H. Woodward. *The Flora of the Unicorn Tapestries.* 2d ed. 1947. Reprint. New York: The New York Botanical Garden, 1974. A pamphlet by two botanists, first published in the *Journal of the New York Botanical Garden* (May–June, 1941). It includes diagrams of the Unicorn Tapestries on which many of the plants are keyed to a corresponding plant list. Although the authors were not able to identify all the plants, this is the most important work on the subject to date.

Amherst, Alicia [Cecil, Hon. Alicia Margaret (Tyssen-Amherst)]. *A History of Gardening in England.* London: Quaritch, 1895. Includes good chapters on monastic gardening, on gardens of the thirteenth, fourteenth, and fifteenth centuries, and on early garden literature.

Anderson, Frank J., ed. *Herbals Through 1500.* The Illustrated Bartsch, vol. 90. 2 vols. New York: Abaris, 1983–84. A monumental study of German herbals from 1400 through 1500. Volume 1 is a picture atlas of plants in printed herbals of the period. Volume 2 comprises commentaries on the uses, folklore, and symbolism of the plants.

_____ . *An Illustrated History of the Herbals.* New York: Columbia University Press, 1977. An entertaining and scholarly study of herbals from the first through the sixteenth century.

Arano, Luisa Cogliati. *The Medieval Health Handbook: Tacuinum sanitatis.* Translated and adapted from the original Italian edition by Oscar Ratti and Adele Westbrook. New York: Braziller, 1976. A study of a group of fourteenth-and fifteenth-century illuminated health handbooks based on a text by an Arabian physician of the eleventh century.

Arber, Agnes. *Herbals: Their Origin and Evolution.* New ed. Cambridge: Cambridge University Press, 1938. Traces the development of the printed herbal in Europe between 1470 and 1670.

Bailey, Liberty Hyde, and Ethel Zoe Bailey. *Hortus Third: A Concise Dictionary of Plants Cultivated in the United States and Canada.* New York: Macmillan, 1978. The standard reference work on plants of the United States and Canada. Since most of the plants in the gardens of The Clois-

91

ters, though European in origin, are now fairly common in the United States, this book is indispensable.

Crisp, Frank. *Medieval Gardens*. 2d ed. New York: Hacker, 1979. First published in two volumes in 1924, this work has now been reissued in one volume. It is valuable mainly for its hundreds of reproductions of illustrations from medieval sources.

Doyle, Leonard J., trans. *St. Benedict's Rule for Monasteries*. Collegeville, Minnesota: The Liturgical Press, 1948. Paper-

back translation of St. Benedict's sixth-century Rule, which regulated monastic life throughout the Middle Ages. A good picture of daily life in a medieval monastery can be reconstructed from its precepts.

Freeman, Margaret B. *Herbs for the Medieval Household*. New York: The Metropolitan Museum of Art, 1979. Entertaining accounts, drawn from medieval sources, of eighty-five herbs popular in medieval times for "cooking, healing, and divers uses." Attractively illustrated with reproductions of woodcuts from early printed herbals.

———. *The Unicorn Tapestries*. New York: The Metropolitan Museum of Art, 1976. Lavishly illustrated study of the Unicorn Tapestries that includes a chapter on the plants and their symbolism.

Gothein, Marie Luise. *A History of Garden Art*. Translated by Mrs. Archer-Hind. 2 vols. London: Dent; New York: Dutton, 1928. Volume 1 includes a good chapter on the gardens of the Middle Ages in the West.

Grieve, Maude. *A Modern Herbal*. 2 vols. 1931. Reprint. New York: Dover, 1971. Includes botanical descriptions, characteristics, growth habits, medicinal properties, uses, folk lore, and histories of over 800 plants.

Harvey, John. *Medieval Gardens*. Beaverton, Oregon: Timber Press, 1981. Detailed survey that includes extensive documentation and bibliography. One noteworthy feature is an appendix with a list of over 250 species of plants mentioned in medieval sources.

Horn, Walter, and Ernest Born. *The Plan of St. Gall*. 3 vols. Berkeley: University of California Press, 1979. Monumental study of the plan of St. Gall with comprehensive discussions of the gardens. An abridged version of the book, *The Plan of St. Gall in Brief*, by Lorna Price (Berkeley, 1982), is available.

Hyams, Edward. *A History of Gardens and Gardening*. London: Dent, 1971. The chapter entitled "The Growth of Gardening in Europe's Middle Ages" is a general introduction to the subject.

Kamm, Minnie Watson. *Old-Time Herbs for Northern Gardens*. 1938. Reprint. New York: Dover, 1971. History, lore, and descriptions of over 200 herbs, many of which grow in the gardens of The Cloisters.

Larkey, Sanford V., and Thomas Pyles, eds. *An Herbal [1525]*. New York: The New York Botanical Garden, 1941. Facsimile and modern edition of an anonymous herbal (commonly known as *Banckes's Herbal*) published in London in 1525 by Richard Banckes.

McLean, Teresa. *Medieval English Gardens*. New York: Viking, 1981. A lively introduction to the subject, but not as scholarly as Harvey, *Medieval Gardens*. Includes extensive bibliography.

Pazzini, Adalberto, and Emma Pirani, eds. *Herbarium: Natural Remedies from a Medieval Manuscript*. New York: Rizzoli, 1980. Beautiful full-color reproductions from the *Theatrum sanitatis*, one of the group of manuscripts treated in Arano, *The Medieval Health Handbook*.

Polunin, Oleg. *Flowers of Europe*. London: Oxford University Press, 1969. Comprehensive field guide to the wild flowers of Europe, many of which are found in the gardens of The Cloisters. Good color photographs.

Power, Eileen, trans. *The Goodman of Paris*. London: Routledge, 1928. Translation of a book of instruction written by a wealthy Parisian burgher of the fourteenth century for his young wife. Includes chapters on gardening and cooking.

Rohde, Eleanour Sinclair. *The Old English Herbals*. 1922. Reprint. New York: Dover, 1971. Engagingly written work on the English herbals from Anglo-Saxon times through the seventeenth century.

Sanecki, Kay N. *The Complete Book of Herbs*. New York: Macmillan, 1974. One of the more informative books on the history and uses of herbs. Includes recipes.

Schetky, EthelJane McD., ed. *Dye Plants and Dyeing: A Handbook*. Plants and Gardens, vol. 20, no. 3. Brooklyn, New York: The Brooklyn Botanic Garden, 1964. A pamphlet that contains articles on all aspects of dye plants and dyeing, including histories and descriptions of the plants and prescriptions for their use.

Stokstad, Marilyn, and Jerry Stannard. *Gardens of the Middle Ages*. Lawrence, Kansas: The Spencer Museum of Art, 1983. Illustrated exhibition catalogue that includes much general information in its introductory essays.

Strabo, Walahfrid. *Hortulus*. Translated by Raef Payne, with commentary by Wilfrid Blunt. Pittsburgh: The Hunt Botanical Library, 1966. Translation of a ninth-century monk's poem about his garden. The book is beautifully designed and printed, and includes a facsimile of the earliest-known manuscript of the poem.

Thompson, Daniel V. *The Materials and Techniques of Medieval Painting*. 1936; Reprint. New York: Dover, 1956. Fasci-nating discussion of the medieval painter's materials, many of which were plants that grow in the gardens of The Cloisters.

Young, Bonnie. *A Walk Through The Cloisters*. New York: The Metropolitan Museum of Art, 1979. A guide to the museum, illustrated with color photographs.

LIST OF ILLUSTRATIONS

The illustrations on pages vi, xiv, 3, 5, 8 (*below*), 9 (*above*), 10, 12 (*above, below*), 13, 14 (*above*), 18 (*above*: Sage, *below*), 20 (*above*), 21 (*below*), 24 (*above*: Saffron), 26, 27 (*above*: Garlic, *center*: Parsley, *below*: Pea), 29, 44 (*below*: Iris), 45 (*below*: Betony), 48, 51 (*above*: Gourd), 54, 57 (*below*: Garlic), 60 (*below*: Saffron), 67 (*above*: Sage), 72, 80, 82, 84, 87, 89, 92 (*below*), 95, and 97 (*below*) are woodcuts from *Das Buch von Pflantzung* by Petrus de Crescentiis, Strasbourg, 1512. Harris Brisbane Dick Fund, 1926   26.100.2

Details of woodcuts from *Das Buch von Pflantzung* appear on pages 6 (*above, below*), 8 (*above*), 19, 20 (*above*: Onion), 32 (*above*), 36 (*above*: Grapevine, *below*), 42 (*above*: Saffron), 45 (*center*), 49 (*above, below*), 52, 55 (*below*), 58 (*below*), 61 (*above*), 64 (*above*), 67 (*below*), 73 (*below*), 75, 88 (*above*), and 91 (*above*).

The illustrations on pages ix (Chamomile), xi, 22, 33, 38, 41, 42 (*below*), 61 (*below*: Strawberry), 63 (*below*: Horehound), 65 (Chamomile), 66 (*below*: Rose), 71, 73 (*above*: Strawberry), 77 (*below*: Madonna Lily), 93, and 96 (*above*) are woodcuts from *Hortus sanitatis*, Strasbourg, Johann Prüss, ca. 1497. The Elisha Whittelsey Collection, The Elisha Whittelsey Fund, 1944   44.7.37

Details of woodcuts from *Hortus sanitatis* appear on pages xiii, 14 (*below*), 21 (*above*), 23, 39 (*below*), 44 (*above*), 46 (*above*), 51 (*below*), 57 (*above*), 63 (*above, center*), 66 (*above*), 68 (*above*), 70 (*above, below*), 77 (*above*), 78 (*below*), 83, 86 (*center, below*), 88 (*below*), 91 (*below*), 94 (*above*), and 97 (*above*).

The illustrations on pages 7, 11, 15, 28, and 34 (*above*) are woodcuts from *Agricultura vulgare* by Piero Crescentio, Venice, 1519. Harris Brisbane Dick Fund, 1934   34.28.1

Details of woodcuts from *Agricultura vulgare* appear on pages 9 (*below*), 32 (*below*), 34 (*below*), 40 (*above*), 45 (*above*), 55 (*above*), 60 (*above*), 64 (*below*), 78 (*above*), 81 (*above*), 85 (*above, below*), 86 (*above*), 92 (*above*), 94 (*below*), and 96 (*below*).

The illustrations on pages 17, 39 (*above*), and 40 (*below*) are woodcuts by Michel Wolgemuth from *Liber chronicarum* (commonly known as *The Nuremberg Chronicle*) by Hartmann Schedel, Nuremberg, Anton Koberger, 1493. Rogers Fund 1921   21.36.145

The illustrations on pages 20 (*below*), 24 (*below*), 50, 53, 68 (*below*: Grapevine), and 90(*below*: Grapevine) are woodcuts from *Der beschlossen Gart des Rosenkrantz Marie* by Ulrich Pinder, Nuremberg, printed for Pinder, 1505. Harris Brisbane Dick Fund, 1931   31.83

The illustration on page 25 is a woodcut from *Der Spiegel der menschlichen Behaltnisse*, Basel, Bernhart Richel, 1476. Harris Brisbane Dick Fund, 1935   35.55

The illustrations on pages 31 (Madonna Lily), 46 (Violet), 59 (Arum), 62 (Juniper), and 74 (Violet) are woodcuts from *Gart der Gesundheit*, Mainz, Peter Schoeffer, 1485. The Elisha Whittelsey Collection, The Elisha Whittelsey Fund, 1944   44.7.15

The illustrations on pages 35 (*above*), and 81 (*below*) are details of woodcuts from *Ces presentes heures à l'usaige de Rome*, Paris, printed by Pigouchet for Simon Vostre, 1498. Rogers Fund, 1918   18.60

The illustration on page 35 (*below*) is a woodcut (restrike), Germany, 15th century. Rogers Fund, 1925

The illustration on page 58 (*above*: Bryony) is a woodcut from *Hebarius i latino cū figuris*, Louvain, Jan Veldener, ca. 1485–86. The Elisha Whittelsey Collection, The Elisha Whittelsey Fund, 1944   44.7.4

The illustration on page 98 is a woodcut from *Kalendar deutsch*, Augsburg, Hans Schönsperger, 1484. Harris Brisbane Dick Fund, 1926   26.56.1